Hints On Light And Shadow, Composition, Etc.: As Applicable To Landscape Painting

Samuel Prout

In the interest of creating a more extensive selection of rare historical book reprints, we have chosen to reproduce this title even though it may possibly have occasional imperfections such as missing and blurred pages, missing text, poor pictures, markings, dark backgrounds and other reproduction issues beyond our control. Because this work is culturally important, we have made it available as a part of our commitment to protecting, preserving and promoting the world's literature. Thank you for your understanding.

HINTS
ON
LIGHT AND SHADOW,
COMPOSITION, ETC.
AS APPLICABLE TO
LANDSCAPE PAINTING.

Illustrated by Examples,

BY

SAMUEL PROUT, F.S.A.
PAINTER IN WATER COLOURS IN ORDINARY TO HER MAJESTY.

"Yet still how faint by precept is exprest
"The living image in the Painter's breast."

A NEW EDITION, WITH ADDITIONAL EXAMPLES.

LONDON:
M. A. NATTALI, 23, BEDFORD STREET, COVENT GARDEN.
MDCCCXLVIII.

NOTICE TO THE SECOND EDITION.

The importance of BREADTH IN LIGHT AND SHADOW, in Landscape painting, has been so generally acknowledged, that it need only be necessary, in presenting a new edition of the "HINTS," to remark, that with the view of rendering the series of examples as complete as possible, two new plates have been added in further elucidation of the rules already laid down.

An artist must consider what is necessary and what unnecessary to express portraiture, and what are the great essentials, of primary importance, in producing a picture. His main effort should be to produce a broad impression of the scene. In its infancy painting only pretended to exact imitation, the truth and precision of which formed its merit, as they do still with the ignorant. "In the human figure it attempted to distinguish the several hairs of the head, and the pores of the skin; and when it aimed at producing anything like landscape, it was by copying, like the Chinese of our day, distinctly every blade in the grass, every leaf in the trees, and every stone or brick in the buildings, which it tried to represent."*

It was soon, however, discovered that this was rather copying what the mind knew to be, from the concurrent testimony of another sense, than what

* Knight on Taste, p. 149.

the eye saw; and that, even had it been practicable to the utmost extent and variety of Nature, it would not have been a true representation of the visible appearance of things:—for the eye, when at a sufficient distance to comprehend the whole of a human figure, a tree, or a building, within the field of vision, sees facts so comparatively minute as the hair, the leaves, and the stones or bricks, in masses, not individually.

The love of what is called fidelity, therefore, or dry, minute, and almost mechanical detail, is far wide of a faithful representation. The young sketcher thinks himself safe in pourtraying what he believes to exist, under the mistaken impression of describing objects truthfully, and '*the whole*' is forgotten. In the very truth of detail, all truth is lost, and the sketch becomes crowded, confused, and unconnected.

Forms should be defined in large masses, and the distinctive features by expressive touches, leaving what to the eye appears indistinct, undefined, or tenderly drawn. The fault is not in drawing what can be seen, but what cannot be seen— not in not seeing enough, but in seeing too much.

De Crespigny Terrace,
   January, 1848.

HINTS

ON

LIGHT AND SHADOW, AND COMPOSITION,

AS APPLICABLE TO

LANDSCAPE PAINTING.

The Writer presumes to offer the following HINTS ON OUTLINE, LIGHT AND SHADOW, AND COMPOSITION, as the basis of his practice, and the result of his experience. They have been thrown together, principally for juvenile inquirers, divested of all technical difficulties, which but too often form insuperable hindrances to their progress. It is a mere attempt to convey instruction, in the simplest manner, and in the plainest language; and, to facilitate the learner's advancement, the accompanying examples are subjoined, that he may acquire a readier and more perfect knowledge of art than can be gained by precept only. More examples are introduced than are actually needed, some of which may, perhaps, be considered unnecessary repetitions of the same principles and effects; but a variety of illustrations will be useful to one or the other of the numerous classes of students, and, if they do not tend further to confirm and familiarize the business of instruction, may, at least, not be unacceptable as auxiliary lessons for practice.

All artists are distinguished by different powers. One arrests the eye at a distance, another solicits a close examination; one excels in landscape, another in buildings, and a third in figures; while each maintains that original character which constitutes his peculiar charm. The rude romantic scenery in which Salvator Rosa delighted; the enchanting aspects of Nature which distinguish the works of Gaspar Poussin; the space, almost measureless,

"Where an hundred realms appear,"

rich in every variety of foliage, seas, and lakes, splendid palaces, and ruined temples, which ennoble the genius of Claude Lorraine,

"Whate'er Lorraine light-touch'd with softening hue,
"Or savage Rosa dash'd, or learned Poussin drew:"

however diversified, their works respectively display intrinsic excellence and peculiar beauties, establishing an undisputed title to their high celebrity.

In art, as in all knowledge, there are no mysteries, no secrets discoverable by genius only. The entrance on every scientific pursuit may appear somewhat uninviting, and the requirements of mechanical labour, combined with close application, discouraging conditions; yet each progressive step will afford ample amends for every exertion in surmounting difficulties, were those difficulties even more formidable than they really will be found.

Want of talent and want of taste are common lamentations and common excuses, but wonders will be achieved by the lowest ability, if assisted by unremitted diligence. "Nothing is denied to well-directed labour; nothing is to be obtained without it." There must be an assiduous, ardent devotedness, with a firmness of purpose, absorbing the whole mind; never rambling, but pursuing one determined object. It is the persevering who leave their competitors behind; and those who work the hardest always gain the most. The essential requisite is *application*,—more unpretending, more modest than *genius*, for which thousands sigh, but immeasurably more valuable, and incontestably more secure and unfailing. On the contrary, natural talent, conscious of its innate powers, often resists discipline, and deems labour superfluous; but the course of a mind so ill-regulated is always eccentric, accomplishing nothing with certainty: it flutters round every object of study, and rests on none.

The youthful aspirant for fame should congratulate himself on the extraordinary advantages which, in the present day, he possesses in commencing his professional career, as every possible source of instruction is accessible to him; but he should be aware, at the outset, that it generally costs years of laborious study to attain eminence; and that, not unfrequently, the best portion of life is employed in collecting sketches and studies, as future materials, and in embracing every opportunity from external Nature and works of art, to enrich the mind with ideas of truth and beauty:

> " Yet know, these noblest honours of the mind,
> " On rigid terms descend."*

As no limits can be set to the fervent aspirations of improvement, so none can

---

* A portfolio of prints, scrupulously selected, is highly advantageous, if not absolutely necessary, as a means of acquiring valuable ideas. It is not disgraceful to art, nor derogatory even to its advanced professors, to accept assistance from the works of others, if they but kindle and assimilate with their own powers. The greatest caution, however, must be exercised *in the selection*, and every example which is not excellent, should be rejected, as whatever is continually seen, unavoidably vitiates or improves the taste; for such is the force of habit, that where wrong impressions have once been admitted, the light of improvement may strive in vain to pierce the cloud which intercepts its rays.

be set to possible attainments. Men of the greatest genius, however admired by others, never satisfy themselves, perpetually conceiving ideas of perfection which they endeavour to realize. "Attempt great things, expect great things;" and the aphorism is daily verified that "he who aims at excellence will be above mediocrity: who aims at mediocrity will fall short of it." Labour must be animated by the spirit of ambition to place every production in the first rank of talent, and invigorated by the possibility of equal success with those gifted individuals who have soared to the highest range of art.

As this volume can offer little more than general observations, embracing only a small portion of art, the theory of perspective is purposely omitted, although it must be remembered that a knowledge of its principles is *absolutely requisite,* as the only safe foundation for practice.

Perspective is generally considered a dry and distasteful study, and a prejudice exists with many against everything like geometrical drawings; but, without a knowledge of its rules, no object can be properly delineated, and their application alone prevents absurdities, and secures symmetry and truth. The study of the science is sometimes pursued in a manner much too laborious in its minute details; volumes are produced, enough to frighten a beginner, raising barriers on the very threshold, over which the timid student hesitates to proceed, discovering, at the outset of his studies, much which appears perplexing and unfathomable. The education of an architect, indeed, demands a thorough knowledge of the principles of Perspective; but many of them cannot be applied to Landscape painting, and it is presumed that all which is essential for this branch of art, lies within a few simple rules, which may be readily taught and easily comprehended, and, when once acquired, can never be forgotten.

Furnished with this preliminary knowledge of Perspective, the learner may proceed in his attempt to give objects their true representation by *outline*, or, in other words, *to draw accurately.** In delineating objects, every part and peculiarity should be expressed with scrupulous exactness and precision, guarding against that confusion and want of character, — that mere senseless scribbling, the work only of a careless hand. The proportions must be examined, and the copy made faithful in every particular; by which means, the eye, accustomed to representations of truth, becomes familiar with those nicer discriminations that distinguish one object from another. Perspective and correctness of outline, to the artist, like perspicuity and grammatical accuracy in the writer, are not so much accessories as pre-requisites. *Correct drawing is essential to every great work of art : nothing can atone for the want of it, as without it all other excellences will be valueless.*†

A fault very observable, especially in beginners, is the practice of introducing *dark touches*, without considering their value and meaning. Such slovenly productions are completely unpardonable, and are, at once, violations of truth and an abuse of talent. This may be illustrated in delineating the profile of a face. The darkest markings should be reserved for the nostril, the mouth, &c.; but place them without thought on the outline, and the effect, or truth, is destroyed. It is the same with every object in Nature, which can only be correctly expressed by reserving the deepest power of colour for the darkest parts, and by discriminating between *those which are dark, and those which are still darker.*

---

* There is a necessary and obvious distinction between *outline*, which only regards form, and *painting*, which is also conversant with colour, effect, composition, and all the great requisites of art, in the highest acceptation of the term, when applied to landscape painting.

† In the earliest works of the best landscape painters, nothing is seen but fidelity, somewhat stiff, and perhaps hard, but they could not find a better method of mastering difficulties, nor a shorter way of accomplishing their aim.

This inattention is generally imbibed at the commencement of instruction, by yielding to that carelessness which hurries onward, but always the wrong way, and unless vigorously and perseveringly resisted, will become a habit, and throw the student irrecoverably out of his road. The eye and the hand must submit to strict discipline; it is one thing to draw, and another to draw accurately.

Rapidity of execution, or, the dashing off a picture in a short time, cannot be designated other than a specious delusive dexterity; a fruitful source of mischief, which commonly runs either into carelessness or degenerates into mannerism, and, unless resolutely abandoned, must lead to the fatal and inevitable results of bad taste and bad drawing, uncorrected mistakes, and settled defects. Every touch of the pencil should have its intent and meaning; and if the artist, from trick or carelessness, insert strokes not significant to his own mind, they never will be intelligible, much less beautiful, or satisfactory to others. It were invidious to point out instances of this most unjustly applauded practice; but it is assuredly one against which the young artist cannot be too often, nor too strictly cautioned. It is especially to be avoided, because *boldness* and *freedom* seldom fail to attract, and are often thought identical with genius.

Rapidity may be, and is desirable, but only when it results from the confidence of knowledge, and is united with correctness. Let it also be remembered, that a comparison of rapid productions, with any effort of pains-taking talent, will assuredly determine their condemnation. Those who are thus ambitious, and seek to attract the gaze of the world—daring to overturn received principles by means of such extravagant practice, cannot secure to themselves more than a short-lived reputation. Their productions may appear, to the uneducated, *new* and *striking*, and a few followers may subscribe to their notions; but it is departing from the great beaten track to travel in a way the most remote, and which never can lead to just or permanent celebrity: it is exhibiting exaggerated representations of Nature, which in no point of view possess excellence, and are scarcely deserving the lowest degree of praise.

There are artists, again, who make *high finishing* their resting place; whose laborious works are ostentatious displays of dexterity, with contracted feelings, injurious both to the profession and reputation of the painter. An excess of labour does but weaken original vigour; and the diversified and vivid, thus overwrought, become dull and monotonous; for "to paint particulars is not to paint Nature, it is only to paint circumstances." Some parts, in every picture, require to be expressed with force; others, there are, subordinate, to be but faintly touched and skilfully slighted; finish and effect being reserved for what is most interesting. The chief business of the artist should be to generalize ideas: he must possess feeling to avail himself of those occasional combinations which embellish, ennoble, and give grace to his subject. The spectator, in surveying a beautiful scene, derives his pleasure, not from the parts taken separately, but from the impression of *an harmonious whole:* for the same reason, minute and elaborately finished pictures never strongly impress the mind, and are but mere curiosities to gratify persons insensible to higher excellences. Poetry does not consist in words alone: there must be sentiment and fancy, combination and arrangement. An analogous principle may be traced in music, and equally so in painting: the minor details are forgotten in the charm produced by the whole.

Few evils are more fatal to success than *mannerism*, where an uniformity of touch or handling is employed throughout. These means and appliances are never veiled,—the poor ambition seems to be little more than an exhibition of forms and touches. An artist should conceal his materials; never should he aim at a worthless display of adroitness; for such practice is utterly at variance with Nature, injurious to the true cultivation of art, and destructive of its grand aim and end.

The practice of *copying* from the works of any master eminent in his own walk, is one of the first steps towards advancement; it imparts facility in handling, as well as the power of imitation; and even a proficient may occasionally profit by this exercise, especially so far as it tends to the education of the eye in respect of a knowledge of colour and form. Copying is, at best, however, but a species of delusive industry, which should not be encouraged beyond this point, as its dangerous tendency is to satisfy without any mental effort. The pencil of the mere copyist is timid, servile, and meagre; mechanically toiling onward to accomplish, at least, only a limited aim; since, to the mere imitator, copying becomes the end instead of being the means. It is invariably true, that all who thus labour will never "ascend" the bright "heaven of invention:" they are deficient in genuine feeling for art, and incapable of producing works of any *originality;* and let it be remembered that, at last, it is but a poor reputation which has not some claim, however feeble, to that high distinction.

The better practice for the student will be to make *companion pictures* of similar subjects, selecting parts only from approved models, and combining them with his own original ideas. Let him fancy how the artist whom he has chosen as his model, would treat the subject, but not chain himself down to a strict imitation of his manner: it is to a similar mind, and not to a similar hand, to which he should aspire: he must, to quote again the words of a real master in his art, no less sound as a preceptor than admirable as an example, not " tread in his footsteps, but endeavour to keep the same road." Thus unfettered, he will develop principles; new and lively perceptions will take precedence of those rules which were only necessary as elementary guides, till at last an acquired taste will create a relish for higher excellences, enabling him

"To snatch a grace beyond the reach of art."

It is not meant to decry or discountenance *rules:* much always depends upon them: they are the scaffolding by which to raise the fabric. "Could we, indeed, teach taste or genius by rules, they would be, as has been remarked, no longer taste and genius." Feeling and principles must co-operate and proceed hand-in-hand: the union of both is necessary to that superiority which neither of them, unaided by the other, can ever produce.

Definitions are said to be always dangerous, but if the remark may be hazarded, TASTE seems to be the power or faculty of distinguishing beauty from deformity, in art and Nature. It is the preference which a rightly constituted mind gives, as it were, intuitively, to one object, or colour, or composition, above another. This preference, or selection of the graceful and beautiful from the bald and defective, may be called *the art of seeing Nature;* as the peculiar attributes of excellence must be felt, and cannot be acquired by *mere* perseverance in drawing, or even by a thorough acquaintance with the rules of art. Nor is taste attained by the bare examination of Nature, or studying theories of art. Works of talent must not be overlooked, but carefully studied; the eye and the judgment must be exercised by repeatedly inspecting the best specimens of the best masters, and cultivating an intimate acquaintance with their excellences, by which discipline, the mind becomes elevated to a high state of refinement. Such as are well instructed in the school of great names, and most conversant with their productions, learn to think something like them, and feel a kindling of that fire which pre-eminently distinguishes them from others.*

* Taste is, probably, in some degree constitutional, and common to all; but is it not generally the progressive, though, perhaps, imperceptible result of experience? By comparison alone do we ever arrive at the knowledge of what is accurate and most perfect in its kind.

COMPOSITION is the grouping and arrangement of pictorial materials, to express the unity of an entire impression. Nothing marks more strongly the invention of the painter, nor more strongly implies talent, than the power of disposing individual parts, so that they are kept subservient to a whole; for it is not the number of objects, nor particular features, which give pleasure and satisfaction, but what is termed *general effect.*

A picture may consist of many parts, and possess a variety of interest; but, instead of being a display of "boastful art," distracting to the eye, the painter skilfully marshals every feature, and prevents the obtrusion of one object to the prejudice of another; creating that unity of design, that essential breadth, which constitutes real excellence, whether it be in composition, or colour, or light and shadow.

The whole design must be clearly conceived before the picture is begun: nothing should be admitted or omitted at random. Each object has, in truth, a place proper for itself, and all that is introduced should be *with an intention.* In the painter's sketch, or study, the treatment, or broad intention, which it is his object to secure, must be strongly expressed, leaving all minute details to be supplied as they may be required, or as they may suggest themselves in the progress of the work.

The feeling how best to dispose of circumstances, or to make those alterations which may be thought necessary to perfect a picture, should be caught from Nature, at *the time of making the sketch.* This is one of the most certain means of improvement, and so important, that no temptation should be an inducement to neglect it. At that time is seen the fitness of combinations to ensure harmony in the composition. Memory must not be trusted to complete at home what can be done, and only well done, on the spot. The artist is then borrowing a leaf from Nature's own book: from the pages of that great Teacher who will enable him to surmount the most formidable difficulties, and place within his reach all her choicest beauties. Every sketch thus made, even though slight, is of more real value than portfolios of *home-finished* drawings, which, however carefully executed, will never possess the freshness and force inseparable from first thoughts. More mischief is done by thus endeavouring to improve upon an original outline, or effect, than the nicest execution can ever compensate.

The forms of composition are infinite in number, but no one is exclusively perfect. *Triangular*, or *pyramidal composition*, has been selected and introduced in some of the following examples, as exemplifying a principle easily understood. It is applicable to almost every variety of subject, and is, perhaps, hardly ever unpleasant to the eye; it may be adopted to advantage where the subject will admit of it, but as there cannot be any general rule, the taste of the artist will be the best and sufficient guide.

The practice of introducing equal quantities on each side of the picture, or large objects in the centre, is very objectionable, and should be, as far as possible, avoided; but when necessary, in order to preserve locality, good feeling will prevent such forms from being obtrusive, or appearing as competitors to the eye; it being bad taste to set up rivals, where the value of one acts against the other.

There is a higher class of composition, and a separate style of art, sometimes called poetical, which is addressed more to the imagination than to the senses, and cannot strictly be called an imitation, as many of its forms are fanciful, and the painter strives

"To polish Nature with a finer hand."

The imagination of the poet must inspire the hand of the painter; for such intellectual excellence can neither spring from consummate practice, nor even from the closest study of Nature: it is fairy ground, whereon few may venture, as every deviation from the exact characters of Nature is to

"Body forth the forms of things unknown,"

and, unless to him who is "of imagination all compact," the probable result will be wild extravagances and ridiculous conceptions, remarkable chiefly as the productions of a mind seduced into a total forgetfulness of truth.

LIGHT AND SHADOW follow composition. They place power in the hand of an artist to sink what is unseemly into obscurity, and to raise features requiring prominence into suitable conspicuousness. There are many painters, particularly in the Dutch school, whose chiaro obscuro is excellent: but the mind should be imbued in the works of Rembrandt, the mighty magician of light and shade, to which his pictures are indebted for all their powerful impressions. And here it may be advised, in the study of this most important branch of art, that the treatment which produces delight should be attentively examined, especially by tracing the progress, or path of light, through the picture, by which means the intention and principle will be easily understood.*

---

* It is recommended that studies of light and shadow should be made in two colours, such as black and white; a variety of tints being a temptation to deviate from effect, and likely to divert the eye from broad and simple treatment.

High authorities in art have insisted on the necessity of having three lights to perfect a picture. Many, again, maintain that light should be of a wedge-form, or triangular: that it should come in at one corner and pass out at another; but the works and opinions of such theorists are frequently contradictory, and prove that the master of many rules speculates in many systems, and is rarely the best practitioner. The fate of a design is exceedingly doubtful when the artist is fearful of transgressing directions which he is led to believe indispensable, and ponders over the exact quantity of two-thirds, three-fifths, or four-ninths of light and shadow. A frigid submission to such decrees infallibly draws off the student from exercising his own eye and senses, and in endeavouring to produce a picture, faultless in every point, his best efforts end but in a dry and miserable failure.

Breadth of light and shadow is a quality too much neglected, and too little felt, without which the highest finishing and most laborious detail will always fail to prove the master-mind or hand; the excellence of light and shadow mainly depending on breadth. It is evident that many artists in the treatment of their subjects (if it may be called treatment) have been unwilling to unite objects as *a mass*, but give to each separately its proportion of light and shadow, so that they form *pictures of parts*, the very opposite of breadth, and frequently, from an erroneous idea that beauties are sacrificed, by being thrown, as it were, under a cloud.

The exact quantity of light and shadow cannot be suggested, as different subjects require different proportions; neither is a fixed division at all necessary. The best practice is to form *one broad mass*—to keep other masses quite subordinate, and particularly to *avoid equal quantities*.

A *point of light*, or a portion, or object strongly relieved, should always be preserved to give clearness and strength to the rest. A similar contrast may be repeated in several parts of the picture; but unless in smaller quantities, the intention will be frustrated: the greatest emphasis being expressed by the strongest and largest proportion of opposition.*

Shadows may be introduced, even where the immediate cause is not discoverable in the picture. Passing clouds authorize the admission of almost every form of shadow that can play on a plane or exposed surface. A scrupulous, and perhaps somewhat conscientious feeling, may object to profit by such circumstances as may be termed fortunate or accidental, because they did not occur when the sketch was made; but such timid spirits never excel, and remain stationary within their own narrow and prescribed limits. The artist must sometimes feel that his subject requires daring to the very verge of probability, without trespassing on the boundaries of possibility: he must consider what treatment would produce the strongest effect, and awake the imagination to conceptions of something surpassing every-day appearances.

Every scene will vary, according to the circumstances under which it arrests attention: the greatest interest frequently arises from happy combinations, either in form, or colour, or effect. There are days, occasionally, particularly favourable for light and shadow; when travelling clouds, gay in sunshine, cast an infinite variety of capricious, and often, striking effects; following each other in such

---

* The point of light, to which allusion is made, is destroyed where decided forms and hard outlines are suffered to remain throughout the picture; for such positive terminations have no existence in Nature, where all the parts blend to form a whole: at the same time an excess of softening is at variance with all force and effect.

quick succession as to elude all rapidity of hand, leaving the memory alone to retrace their fleeting beauties.

Light and shadow may be studied to the greatest advantage by *moonlight* when the train of light is more clearly traced, and more positive than in sunshine. In obedience to the poet's well known advice, buildings, particularly, may best be seen in the "pale moonlight." It is not only "fair Melrose" which should then be visited by those who would wish to "see it aright," for ruins of such exquisite architecture must be beautiful at all times, and under every diversity of effect; but edifices of far inferior beauty, if their outline and general form be good, will then start forth into prominence, while all the inelegant details, which in "garish day" offend the eye, will be softly mellowed into one grand and harmonious whole. Travellers have come away from a moonlight view of the Coliseum with vivid admiration, such as no daylight visit ever inspired: and let all who wish to pay just homage to the genius of our unrivalled WREN, pace round and about his magnificent temple at the same still and solemn hour, and the grandeur and unity of his design will leave an impression never before experienced, and never to be forgotten. The characteristics of moonlight are the essential requisites of good effect; such as concentrated brilliancy, with smaller glittering lights, large masses of shadow, and a point of light opposed to the deepest shade, while all the minor details become invisible, and sink in the simplicity and grandeur of the whole.

The purpose of art is to represent objects with gracefulness and truth; and much of the charm of a picture depends on the skilful management of *contrast*, both in form and colour. It is not to be effected by violent *contrarieties*, but by varying the direction of lines, and by diverting the eye from positive forms: a burst of light across a mass of shade, or shadows shooting over the breadth of light, to separate one part from another, shew the power of opposition. All, however, must appear natural, unforced, never destroying that *repose* which is required in every picture:

"Truth owns but one direct and perfect line."

There must be a variety, but there must be *a whole;* without *simplicity* no composition can be complete, and the most skilful representation of Nature will degenerate into pedantry and affectation.

In the arrangement of accessories to complete the picture, nothing should be admitted which disturbs the composition; all must be appropriate and in accordance with the intended effect. The interest of the spectator can only be commanded by the unity of the whole.

Whatever be the objects thus introduced, the question should be: If they were placed differently, what composition would best express the intention? Frequent exercises of this kind will improve taste, and although arrangements may be entirely dissimilar (for what one artist admits another will reject), yet they will appear equally pleasing. At the same time, as has been stated before, there must be a *purpose* throughout the design, without which all will be misplaced.

REMARKS ON THE EXAMPLES.

It was found impossible in the following observations to avoid recapitulating what has been said before, but the same principles must be exercised in every variety of subject.

In pursuing the study of arrangement, good feeling may be acquired by stripping the subjects of such additional objects as are introduced to make the picture, by which means it will be ascertained if they produce the effect intended; or, if it is not possible to substitute another composition possessing greater advantages; for it must be remembered, that "it cannot be by chance, that excellences are produced with any constancy or any certainty, for this is not the nature of chance."

Pl.1

PLATE I.

Examples are given of the same scene, as far as regards the outline, but varied in treatment. In No. 1, the boat and figures nearly occupy the centre; some object, equally *dark* and *light*, therefore, was necessary, *in a less quantity*, to prevent the principal group from appearing as if by itself, and unconnected with the whole. In the example No. 2, the mass of rock in the foreground is repeated in the same manner and with the same intention, the smaller quantity being opposed to the larger. In Nos. 6 and 7, light and shadow are respectively interchanged by way of contrast, but in similar proportions, and conducted from the buildings to the boats, which, with the awnings, &c. connect the separate parts, break the continuity of line, secure *breadth*, and preserve throughout the interest of the picture.

The treatment ought always to be governed by the character of the scene: many subjects are most striking under a cloudless sky, or wrapt in the grey tones of twilight; others, again, are best represented with force and decision, both of light and shadow, or colour.

The centre subjects illustrate what is meant by *masses* of light and shadow, and *points of light*, or small quantities introduced with the strongest opposition. Page 14.

PLATE II.

Contains examples of the broadest and simplest treatment, in which the upright lines are broken and relieved by bold angular shadows and bright lights. No. 3 is represented in the deepest shadow, with a burst of strong light, which is repeated, only in small quantities, that the *breadth* of effect may not be disturbed: nothing should be introduced, and everything must be sacrificed, which diminishes this very important quality.

Strong effects are easily produced by surrounding any particular portion with the greatest quantity of shadow, but such violent contrast, unconnected by gradations, will always appear artificial; watchful care is required to avoid a taste for extremes, and in the *use* of light and shadow, let it always be remembered that *darkness* is not necessarily " *depth.*"

PLATE III.

Furnishes examples of large parts and decided forms; and, while precision should be studiously preserved, it must pervade without hardness of outline, for too great a repetition of strong dark, in contact with strong light, will destroy repose. (See Plate V.)

Breadth is a technical term of art, frequently employed so indiscriminately, and applied to express ideas of such different natures, as to render any attempt to limit its meaning, within the strict and narrow boundaries of generally satisfactory definitions, exceedingly difficult. The common acceptation of the term is, an extension of light, dark, or half light: the quantity expressing different degrees of the character of effect required.

Simple objects are best calculated to exemplify the advantages of this mode of treatment and arrangement, which, when once felt, may be successfully tried on every variety of subject.

Pl. IV.

PLATE IV.

No. 1. THE RIALTO AT VENICE. The light and shadow are in large masses, with smaller quantities diffused over the shipping and figures, conveying the interest and animation of the scene through the picture, preventing the appearance of boundaries to each, and connecting the intermediate parts. The group in the foreground was required to express distance, but it would too much have diminished the importance of the bridge and buildings, if their magnitude had not been securely indicated by the small boats and figures immediately under them. No. 2 is another example of breadth of effect, which is the first quality to be secured, for it is the basis on which the additional interest of the picture can alone be sustained. Light is carried into the shadow by figures, and similar objects express the same intention on the opposite side, and prevent the eye from resting on any part of the scene.

Pl V

2

PLATE V.

No. 1. AT VENICE. The broad square mass of light on the palace, is repeated in an inferior mass on the column and boats. Small objects, and reflections, as connecting links, lead the light across the picture, round to the busy incidents in the foreground, which, as points of the strongest opposition, heighten the brilliancy of the scene, and give distance to the buildings. The accidental circumstances and animation which characterize commerce, are preserved throughout, but in this, and in Plate IV., No. 1, a necessary space for *repose* is reserved on the water, as bustle, without some proportionate degree of calmness and quiet, must inevitably be fatal to good effect.

Every accompaniment, in every view, should be locally correct, and only introduced to aid in producing altogether an harmonious and picturesque whole.

The management in No. 2, is also in the broadest manner: the awning on the shadowed side of the house, assisted by the mast of the boat, connect the light on both buildings, which is carried out of the picture by the drapery and figures.

Shadows will be heavy and monotonous, unless portions of light, or half light, are conveyed into them, without destroying breadth.

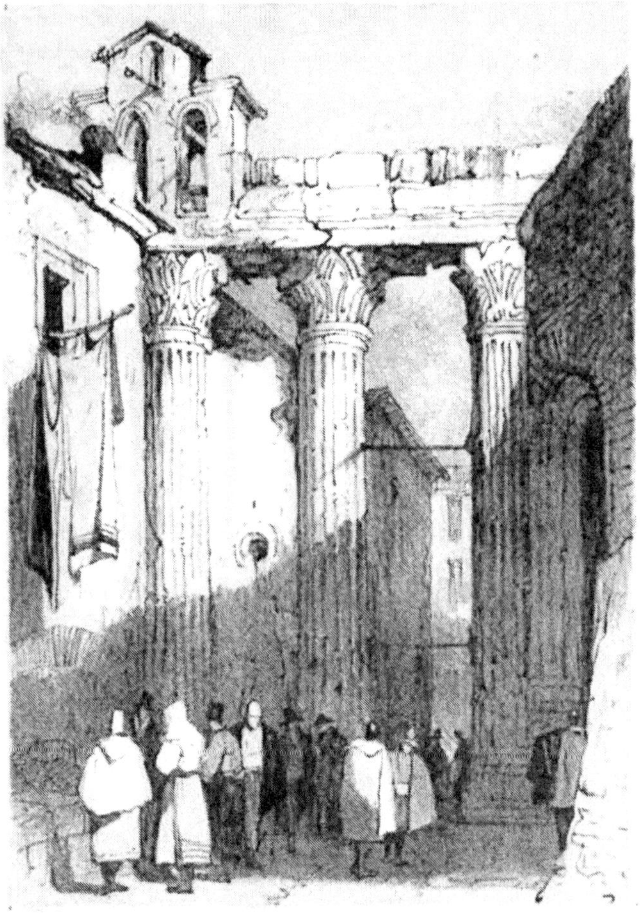

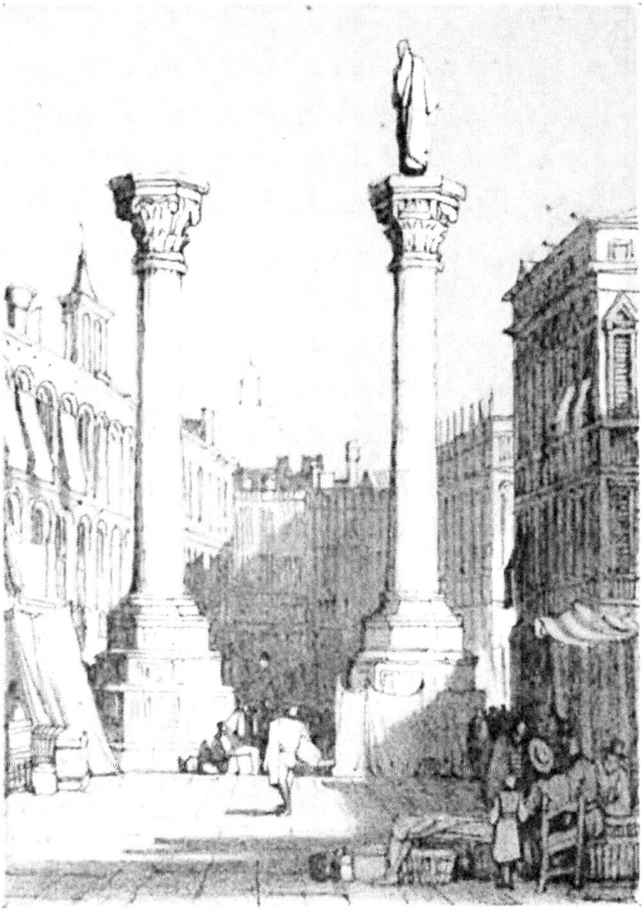

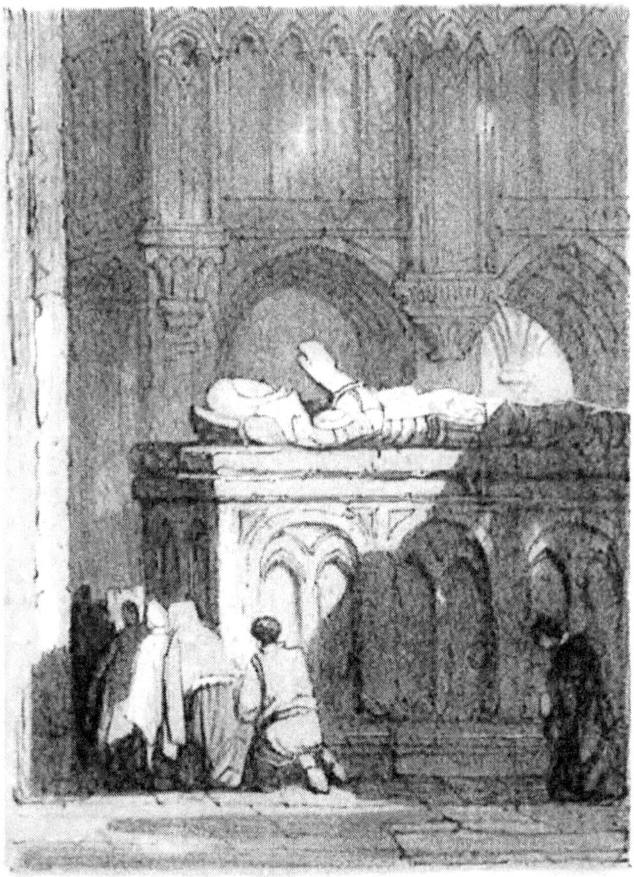

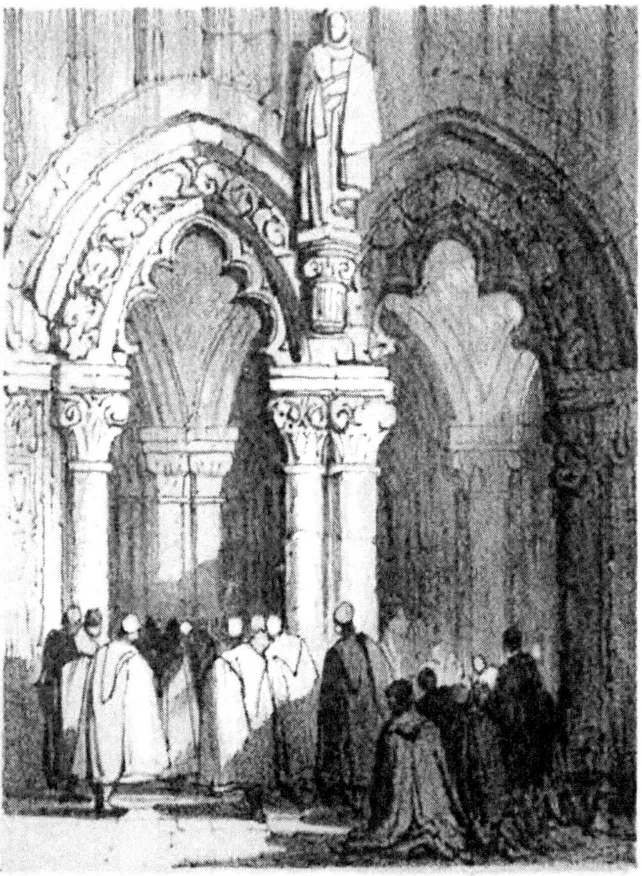

PLATE VI.

These examples explain the remarks which were made on the introduction of figures, or of other objects, *to increase breadth*. The light and dark should, as it were, travel about the picture; but unless they are intimately, yet almost imperceptibly blended (while the predominance, nevertheless, of one mass over another is never sacrificed), there will be a hardness, and an affectation in the treatment. As the subjects are composed of many perpendicular lines (which must not be obtrusively seen), the intersecting shadows, reflected lights, and various casual incidents, intermingling throughout, assist to disguise the repetition of these similar forms, without disturbing their simplicity.

It would be tedious to point out every detail, and the nice, and seemingly unimportant particulars on which the interest depends. Feeling, and observation, and taste, must, in these matters, be the instructors. Let it, however, be always remembered that positive forms, and harsh, *cutting* outlines, are contrary to truth and beauty, and should never force themselves on the eye, except in small proportions, to produce solidity, and what is termed a point of light. (Page 14.)

Pl. VII.

PLATE VII.

No. 1. The light on the upper part of the sky, by uniting with the distant columns, gives *breadth* to the composition. Accidental angular shadows (page 14) assist in increasing the proportion of dark, and hide the otherwise unpleasant quantity of perpendicular and parallel lines: for although the repetition of lines may constitute a great beauty in the picture, circumstances should be introduced to divert the eye from the mere recurrence of forms. If a smaller proportion of light had not been brought into the foreground, the shadow and light would have been too much equally divided. In the accompanying Venetian subject, the light enters from the building on the left, and conducted by an awning to the craft and figures, and again by drapery, falls into the full mass of sunshine.

The objects may appear to have been placed too artificially, but here, as in several of the examples, it has not been attempted to hide the art; on the contrary, it has purposely been made as evident as possible, that it might be the more clearly seen and understood.

Pl. VIII

PLATE VIII.

The first scene is little more than a back ground for the vessels. Had it been designed to give importance to it *as a view*, smaller objects in the middle distance, of the same character, would have opened the space, and given additional prominence to the principal feature. Without the distant vessel, the castle and shipping would have been in equal quantities, and the composition ungracefully divided: and had not the smaller boat with figures been added, the vessels, as well as the light, must have appeared disjointed and unconnected.

It has been before recommended as excellent practice, to substitute other features in the same, or another arrangement, but it must be recollected as a fixed rule, that the eye should never be tempted to *count* objects: they must never seem totally separated and disunited, but be made to appear in some way combined as a *whole*.

In the lower example there are two masses of light, connected by smaller portions, carried across to the figure in the foreground, which is the point of light, and intended to give distance.

Pl. IX

PLATE IX.

The preceding remarks are equally applicable to these illustrations. In No. 1, the near boat and the buoy answer to the distant and nearer vessels: and in No. 2, if the larger boat had not been grouped with the more distant one, it would have appeared an isolated feature in the middle of the picture. Nos. 3 and 4 are examples of the strongest opposition, exhibiting the extreme power of light and shadow, and confining the attention to one particular circumstance.

The character of an object, or the circumstance to be expressed, must be preserved predominant; and it is of the utmost consequence to remember, that whatever attracts attention from the principal feature, weakens and disturbs the strength of its expression.

Pl X

PLATE X.

These examples are to enforce the rule, which cannot be too often repeated, that, where two or more masses of light or shadow are introduced, they must not be of equal quantities (page 13); the proportion of contrast in No. 3 is seldom admissible, but some object, strongly opposed by light and shadow, gives vigour, and is especially valuable in producing clearness to the middle-tints.

If the single figure in No 5 had been more to the right, it would have been too much *disunited* from the principal light: and equally out of place, or too near, if it had been immediately under it. The intention is to *repeat* both the *light* and the *dark*, and lead them into the foreground. The figures, and accessories, in the other examples, are placed to preserve that *balance* of subject, which is essential to good composition. Were the figure omitted in the centre view, nearly half the picture would be without interest, and the light on the building a mere spot. Smaller objects, in light, on the middle distance, would have answered the same purpose.

Pl. XI.

PLATE XI.

No. 1. The lines of the sea and distance are diverted by vessels, and the parallel line of the boat is lost in a shadow casually passing over it; and the bright light on the water, assisted by the opposition of shadow, mingling the several forms agreeably together. No. 2 is a range of Martello towers, of the same size and form, in bright light, which repetition would have appeared exceedingly unpicturesque, and far too prominent, if not broken by the effect of an *accidental shadow*, which is often invaluable to the painter, and such accidents may be seen daily, by every one who studies Nature's exhaustless volume of instruction (page 14). Dark and light parts are supposed to enter the picture at the horizon, and pass along the shore, on a curved line, to the nearest objects. This *line*, or method of arrangement, is one of the secrets, if they may be so called, of "*picture-making*," and unless it is felt, and adopted, the best materials are of little value. Any *particular* line, or rule, may not be applicable to all subjects, but some such principle is necessary, to avoid confusion. There must be plan, and system, *a previous conception in the mind*, or there will be no good effect; and it is better to be too artificial than apparently to work, as it were, by random or by chance (page 10). In No. 3, the principal interest is concentrated, but the small boat and distant figure are sufficient to prevent the chief object from appearing detached.

Pl.XII

PLATE XII.

In the first subject, the forms of the bathing-machines are, by themselves, objectionable, and, to adapt them for a picture, the introduction of some additional circumstance was necessary to increase the interest: the single figure is essential to lead off the attention from the centre group. In No. 2 the quantity of small parts, and similar forms, required both contrast and repose. Drapery is hung up for that purpose, and the larger figures are meant to divert the eye from the parallel lines of the buildings, and extend the interest of the scene to the foreground. Baskets, or any appropriate picturesque objects, would have answered the same purpose. Each example illustrates the principle, that figures, colour, forms, &c., *should be repeated*, only in smaller degrees, and that equal interest, or any *equal* quantities, will distract the eye: one must be made to predominate over the rest.

Pl. XIII

PLATE XIII.

In the first example, the light on the temple is connected by drapery with light on the foreground, without which the different parts would have been too much detached. In No. 4, light and shadow are kept broad; figures repeat the upright lines of the broken columns, and prevent their becoming obtrusive and separated features. The subject at Venice, No. 2, is in full light, with only a small proportion of half tint to relieve the buildings from the sky. In the arrangement of figures, it has been attempted to express space, and to unite the detached parts by various groups. No. 3 exemplifies the greatest breadth of light and shadow, with the repetition of each in small quantities, for the purpose of carrying one into the other, and leading the attention through the picture, otherwise the division would appear too strongly defined; displaying the art, which it is always necessary, in a degree, to obscure.

Pl. XIV

PLATE XIV.

The three marine subjects are examples of *broad, or large forms*. The difficulty is to avoid extremes between a multiplicity of parts, which destroy solidity and effect, and large, solitary, unbroken masses, which look bald, and are an affectation, or a caricature of breadth. Although every picture should possess a leading feature, in these examples, (considered as pictures,) the boats are too principal, and a greater quantity of space is required, with additional objects of less interest, which should be arranged as in Plate XVI. In the two centre subjects, the figures, and other accessories, at once connect the light and shadow, and vary the lines, preserving in one the largest proportion of light and the other of shadow. The lower examples are different proportions of light and shadow: in the first, light is principal; shadow, in the second; and half-light in the third; with a point of light in each.

Pl. XV.

PLATE XV.

No. 1. The bright light, and the various objects introduced, are led through the picture to the boats in the foreground, which group, it must be observed, is essential, not only to form a *mass* of additional interest, and to give distance, but to divert the eye from the straight line of the bridge, which, otherwise, would have appeared too obtrusive. In No. 2, the towers, being detached and prominent features, accessories were required to unite them, as parts of a whole; and without the foreground figures, there would have been an equal vacant space at each termination of the boats. In the three smaller examples, groups of figures are combined with scenes, and made principal, to illustrate what has been enforced throughout the previous examples, that, whatever are the component parts of a picture, they must never appear of equal quantities.

Pl.XVI

PLATE XVI.

Is an application of the foregoing principles to a different class of subject.

The composition is pyramidal, but the intention is particularly to shew that the most pleasing and successful effects are those resulting from an arrangement of parts, on different lines : there are certain lines which possess a greater degree of beauty, and are more applicable to one subject than another, but in every subject the eye will be displeased, and the feelings disturbed, where objects have not been *composed*. (See Plate XI.)

The vessels are arranged on an ellipsis, and it will be seen, in both examples, that unless this line of objects be continued from the horizon to the fore-ground, the picture will be incomplete, and that, without the near boats, the distance would press too much on the eye, and hang over the fore-ground.

Further illustrations of this method of disposing of a quantity of circumstances will be seen in the groups of figures, Plates XVIII. and XX.

Pl XVII

Pl. XVIII.

Pl XIX.

Pl XX.

Four plates of figures are added, as further illustrations of the preceding principles of composition and effect.

Let it be clearly and distinctly enforced, that, in every figure and group, *large forms* and *breadth* must never be sacrificed; light being united to light, and shadow to shadow, to create a sufficient and pleasing proportion of each, as in Plates XVII. and XIX.

In disposing of a number of figures, each should have its proper place, and *always in reference to a whole*, for on such combinations the effect will entirely depend, and without this forethought and consideration, the greatest diligence in finishing, or beauty in colour, will be in vain. There should always be one principal group, and smaller groups, with here and there detached figures, to express distances and render the composition and effect more picturesque. It has often been repeated that, without some scheme of arrangement, an assemblage of objects will only be confused, and the very number and diversity of parts will but perplex and bewilder the eye. In the market scenes, Plates XVIII. and XX., the figures are placed on a *curved*, or elliptical line, maintaining the strongest opposition between objects in the distance and the foreground; which, although by no means a general rule, is frequently an agreeable and effective contrast. The same arrangement will be discovered in several of the previous examples, as well as the same *pyramidal composition* recommended at page 11.

The student must keep in mind, that there are parts in every picture to be kept subordinate, or good effect is unavoidably destroyed. This is, perhaps, the greatest difficulty he has to encounter and overcome, and the most difficult subject on which to offer directions, as the treatment must emanate from circumstances, and can only be governed by sentiment and taste.

Pl. XXI.

PLATE XXI.

The principle of breadth applies to figures, which, carelessly introduced, are useless, or rather destructive of good effect.

Hints have already been offered respecting *arrangement*, and the necessity of *an intention*. Single figures, or groups, derive their value from being rightly placed, so as to combine in perfect harmony with the scene, forming parts of a whole. They must be interwoven with each other, appropriate and locally characteristic, never admitting extraneous or accidental circumstances which attract particular attention.

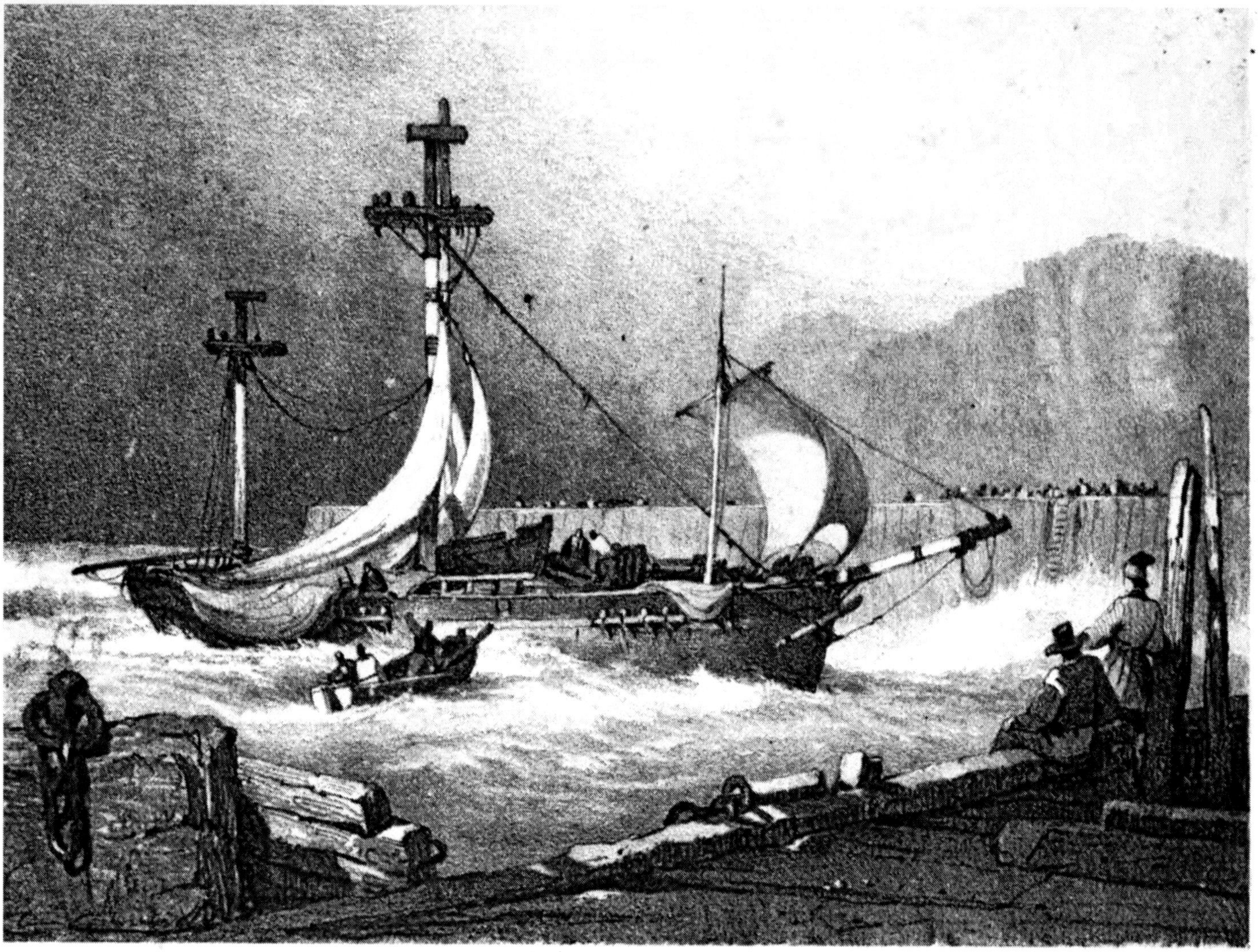

2

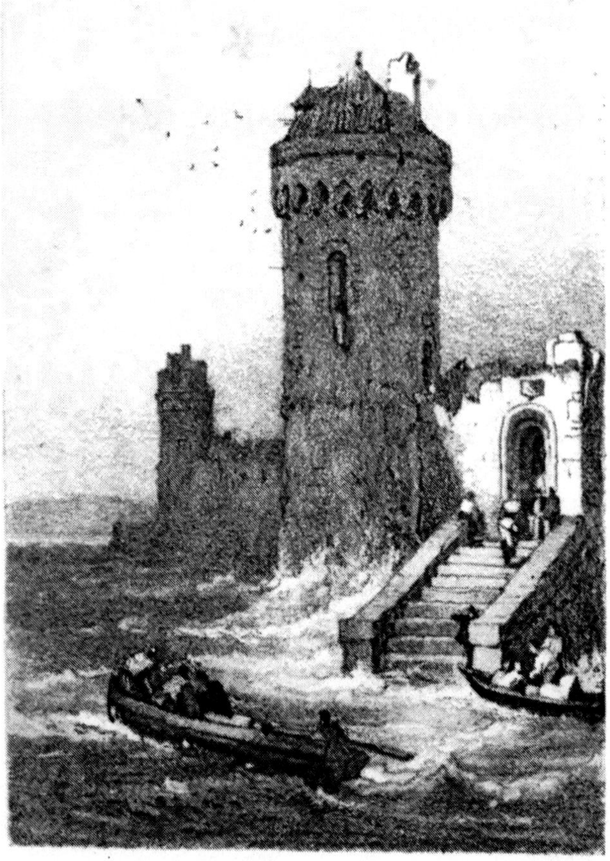

3

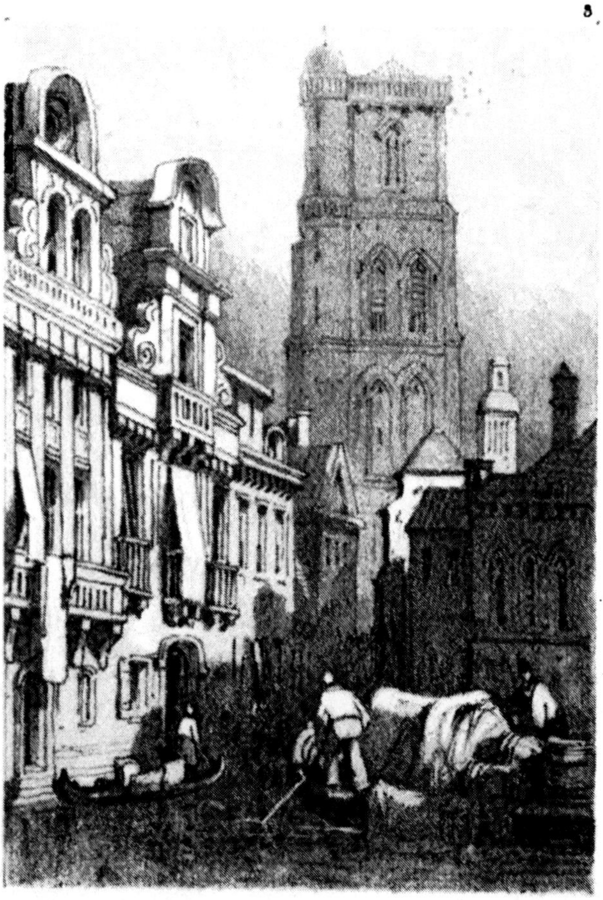

PLATE XXII.

Illustrates how an association of circumstances may be made to excite a stronger sensation than if simply represented as a fact, and perfectly true.

Probably, when the sketch was taken, the wreck was seen entering the harbour under a bright and cloudless sky, and no particular impression was made on the spectator, beyond the event. But, would not a fearful dark cloud, and an agitated sea, immediately describe the cause, and become necessarily associated with the wreck? Would they not be in perfect harmony as a whole? demonstrating the value of *imagination*.

An artist's mind must be conscious of an effort to obtain an end beyond what is common place, yet not misled by visionary conceptions, and exaggerated representations, determining every thing by reason and truth, all consistent and in perfect harmony.